D0532892

SCOTT SIMPSON

BLACK & WHITE PUBLISHING

First published 2004
by Black & White Publishing Ltd
99 Giles Street, Edinburgh EH6 6BZ

Reprinted 2004, 2005, 2007

ISBN 13: 978 184502 036 1

ISBN 1 84502 036 7

British Library Cataloguing in Publication Data:
A catalogue record for this book is available
from the British Library.

Cover illustration by Scott Simpson

Printed and bound by Nørhaven Paperback A/S

Special thanks to Dave Stewart whose encyclopaedic knowledge of neds, ice cream vans and marbles made this book what it is.

Thanks must also go to John Abernethy, Campbell Brown, Shona Moir, Charlie Thompson and Liz Thorburn for their contributions, guidance and support.

And finally a big thank you to Neil McLaughlin and Billy Owens for giving me a well deserved fit up the erse.

SS

A

Arab

A supporter of Dundee United Football Club. The team themselves are also known as The Arabs and is a reference to the once sandy condition of the pitch at Tannadice, the team's home ground.

Arse Bandit

A politically incorrect and deeply offensive term for a homosexual man. In certain circles the insult is not exclusively reserved for homosexuals and can be broadened to incorporate men who own an item of pink clothing, read books or know how to use a knife and fork.

Arsed

Bothered. If you cannot be **arsed** to do something it simply means you cannot be bothered.
*"I was supposed to visit ma **auld dear** in hospital the night but I cannae be **arsed**."*

Auld Dear/Auld Man

Mother and Father. Mothers can also be referred to as **The Auld Dutch, Maw or Ma**.

Auld Firm Game

A meeting of the two Glasgow clubs, Celtic and Rangers. The match usually consists of 90 minutes of sectarian chanting and death threats and it is not uncommon for some football to take place at the same time.

Auld Reekie

Up until the late 19th century, Edinburgh was infamous for its thousands of smoke belching chimneys and open sewers. This earned the city this unenviable nickname, which quite literally means Old Smoky.

Auld Yin

An affectionate term for anyone older than yourself.

Away An Bile Yer Heid

Taken literally this means 'Go Away And Boil Your Head.' It is a phrase which expresses disbelief or dismissal. Similar sentiments can be expressed in the following: **Aye Ma Auntie, Away And Cuddle Ma Humph, Yer Erse Fell Off** or the ever popular **Away And Fling Shite At Yersel.**

Awfy

Means both awful and awfully.
*"That was **awfy** what happened to that wee **laddie** thit got run over by that car."*
*"That was an **awfy** big car that hit that wee **laddie**."*

B

Back Green

The communal garden or drying area found to the rear of most tenement buildings. As well as being used for drying washing, **back greens** are used by children playing and for the storage of broken white kitchen appliances.

Backie

To give someone a **Backie** is to allow them to ride pillion on a bicycle or motorbike.

Baffies

Slippers. **Baffies** are normally tartan, sheepskin and have a wee zip at the side.

Baggie

A minnow.
*"We're away tae the burn tae catch **baggies**."*

Baggsie

To claim something for yourself.
*"I **baggsie** first drink oot that bottle."*

Bahookie

One's backside. Also known as a **Doup**, **Erse**, **Erky**, **Hole** or **Jacksy**.

So the man who exposed himself to you is described as being between 30 and 35 years of age, slim build, pale complexion and has a walloper like a bairn's airm haudin an apple.

Baigie Heid
A severe headache brought on by heavy drinking the night before. A hangover.

Bairn
Scots dialect for a child.

Bairn's Airm Haudin An Apple
A flattering description of a well endowed gentleman's wedding tackle.
*"Big Al might have had a face like a blind cobbler's thumb but he had a **walloper** like a **bairn's airm haudin an apple**."*

Bairn With A Biscuit Arse
A hypothetical child who is more than capable of undertaking the simplest of tasks and employed to illustrate the shortcomings of others.
*"So they've written a book about Scottish slang? So what? **A bairn with a biscuit arse** could have done that."*

Balloon
An insult directed towards someone who is full of hot air.
"That Tony Blair's nothin but a balloon."

Ballop
The flies on a pair of trousers.
*"How embarrassing – my **ballop** appears to be open."*

Baltic

To be freezing cold.
"Shut that windae – it's baltic in here."

Bam

A nutter.
"Shut up, ya bam!"
There are several other words one might use to suggest that someone is of lower than normal intelligence, including **Dafty**, **Dingul**, **Doss**, **Dooboo**, **Dough-Heid**, **Dunderheid**, **Galoot**, **Gowk**, **Numptie** or **Pie**.

Banjo

To strike someone
*"He called my wife a **howk** so I **banjoed** him."*
Also **Blooter**.

Bar

Unit of currency equivalent to one pound.

Barkit

A north-east word meaning very dirty.

Bar-L

Nickname for Barlinnie Prison in Glasgow.
Also known as **The Big Hoose Wi The Wee Windaes** or **The Riddrie Hilton**.

Barley

A word cried out by children during a game to call for a break in play.
Also **Keys-Up**.

Barney

A loud noise or disturbance normally caused by some kind of argument or altercation.

Also **Rammy** or **Stramash**.

Barras

The famous Glasgow flea market where keen eyed bargain hunters can pick up anything from a genuine Charles Rennie Mackintosh tea strainer to a poor quality DVD of the latest Hollywood blockbuster.

Barry

A common Edinburgh expression for anything good or enjoyable.

*"The Deep Sea dae a **barry** fish supper."*

Baw Bag

1. The scrotum. **2.** An insult used to describe someone who is of low moral fibre.

*"Did ye hear aboot auld Mrs Gow? Some **baw bag** mugged her on the way back from bingo and **chored** her winnins."*

Baw Deep

Descriptive term for how sexually active a young man has been.

*"I was **baw deep** wi that burd fae Leith last night."*

Baw Face

Someone with a fat and/or round face.

Baw Hair

Small yet non-specific measurement. A hair's breadth
"That car just missed me by a baw hair."

Baw Heid

One whose head resembles a football, if not in shape then in content.

Baws

Balls = testicles.

Beamer

A red face caused by shame or humiliation.
"My auld dear found a rake of scuddy books under my scratcher and I took a right beamer."
Also **Riddy**.

Beast

A sex offender ie rapist or child molester. The segregated unit of a prison in which sex offenders are incarcerated is known as the **Beast** wing.

Bellywasher

Beer or lager.

Besom

A **besom** is an old Scots word for a broom but it is now chiefly used to describe a cheeky or unruly person.

Bevvy

1. Any alcoholic beverage. **2.** To consume alcoholic beverages.

Bhoy

A supporter of Celtic Football Club.

Bidie In

A common law wife or husband.
*"She's no his wife, she's just his **bidie in**."*

Big Tam

The famous Hollywood actor Sean Connery is better known in his home town of Edinburgh as **Big Tam**. Connery once worked as a milkman and, according to Edinburgh folklore, his round was almost as long as Santa Claus's.

Big Yin

In his home town of Glasgow, the comedian and actor Billy Connolly is better known as the **Big Yin**. This literally means Big One.

Billy Boy

A protestant. **Billy Boys** take their name from King William of Orange who defeated the catholic army at the Battle of the Boyne in 1690.

Binger
A lost bet on a horse race.

Bin Raker
An insult aimed at someone of a scruffy or untidy appearance to suggest that they root through garbage in search of food and clothing.
Also **Bin Howker**.

Bins
Spectacles.

Bit
The house, street or general area in which you reside.
*"I met a crackin lookin burd at Reflections last night and we ended up going back to my **bit**."*

Black Affrontit
To be shocked and offended by someone or something.
*"The priest came roond for his tea last night and wee Jimmy told him to piss off. I was **black affrontit**, so I was."*

Blaud
To be spoiled, ruined or damaged.

Blaw
Cannabis.

Blether

1. One who talks incessantly, normally about nothing in particular. 2. To talk incessantly about nothing in particular.

"Och, quit yer bletherin."

Also **Blatherskate**.

Blob

A condom.

"I could have been baw deep wi that lassie but I didnae huv a blob on me."

Also **Wellie**.

Blootered

To be in a state of advanced intoxication. Also **Beelin**, **Cabbaged**, **Fleein**, **Fu**, **Hammered**, **Guttered**, **Miraculous**, **Nuggets**, **Pie-Eyed**, **Pished**, **Reekin**, **Steamin**, **Steamboats**, **Stocious** and **Wellied**.

Bluenose

A supporter of Glasgow Rangers Football Club, blue being the team's colours.

Boaby

1. Shortened form of the man's name Robert. 2. A penis. 3. A policeman. If, for example, you were recounting a tale in which the police arrested a man called Robert for exposing himself, you might say

"The boaby's lifted Boaby fur flashin his boaby."

Boak

To vomit. To go through the motions of being sick without actually doing so is to get the **Dry Boak**. Also **Heave**, **Spew** or **Shoutin oan Hughie**.

Body Swerve

To avoid someone, or a situation, is known as giving them, or it, a **body swerve**.

Bogey

1. Nasal debris. **2.** A home made go-kart constructed from discarded pieces of timber and an old set of pram wheels.
Also **Guider** or **Cairtie**.

Boggin

Descriptive term for an unpleasant taste or aroma. Can also mean dirty.
"The toilets in the Clachan are boggin."

Bools

Marbles. Different types of marbles include **Onesies**, **Twosies**, **Yogies**, **Chinkies**, **Steelies**, **Stainies**, **Eggies**, **Spacies** and **Glessies**.

Bools In The Mooth

If someone has **bools in their mooth** it means they speak with an upper-class accent.

Bonnie

Beautiful.

"That lassie is awfy bonnie."

Bosie

An embrace or a cuddle.

"Come and gie yer granny a wee bosie."

Bothy

A small room, shed or portakabin where workmen drink tea, read newspapers and play cards.

Also **Howf**.

Bowff

Description of something that tastes foul.

"This soup is bowff."

Brass Nail

A prostitute.

Also **Hoor**.

Brammer

If something is a **brammer** it is very good or impressive.

"Yer new car's a brammer."

Breeks

Trousers.

"Look at that daft wee laddie running around with no arse in his breeks."

Breenge
To lunge forward in a clumsy and thoughtless manner.

Breid
Bread. In the North of Scotland it can also mean oat cakes.

Brian Donlevy
Rhyming slang for a pint of heavy.

Brocher
An inhabitant of the town of Fraserburgh.

Brock
Rubbish, garbage or debris.
*"The builders left a **rake** of **brock** in the **back green**."*

Bubble
To cry in such a way that large green bubbles of snot appear from one's nose.

Buckie
A type of shellfish similar to a winkle which is boiled in salt water, soaked in vinegar and eaten straight from the shell with the aid of a pin.
Also **snotters in crash helmets**.

Bucky

Short for Buckfast. A tonic wine with a high alcohol content manufactured by the Benedictine monks of Buckfast Abbey in Devon. 80% of their gross annual sales are made in the Strathclyde area.

Buggery

As well as its universal meaning, **buggery** is also a mythical destination to which anyone who displeases you is instructed to go.
*"Get you away to **buggery**!"*

Bumfelled

If something is described as **bumfelled** it means it has a crease or ruck in it
*"Och wid ye look it ma cairpet, it's aw **bumfelled**."*

Bump

To **Bump** someone is to abandon them or to refuse to pay back a debt.

Bumpin Yer Gums

Talking about nothing in particular.

Bunker

The work surface next to the kitchen sink.
*"Just leave those dirty dishes on the **bunker**."*

Bunnet

A flat cap commonly worn by pensioners.
Also **Cadie**.

Bunnet Hustler

A derogatory term for someone of upper or middle class who pretends to be working class.

*"That new shop steward likes to kid himsel oan thit he's one ay us, but he's just another **bunnet hustler**."*

Burd

A common term for any woman.

Buroo

The social security office where unemployed people make a fortnightly trip to sign on the dole. Sometimes known in Glasgow as **The Parish**.

Burst Couch

An unflattering description of someone who is both overweight and unattractive.

*"Michelle's a nice enough lassie but she looks like a **burst couch**."*

Burst Mooth

An injury received when one is punched in the mouth. A fat lip.

C

Cadge
To scrounge.
"Can I cadge a lift up the road?"
Also **Mooch**.

Cairry Oot
Alcohol purchased from an off-licence for
consumption at home, a party or a park bench.
Also **Cargo**.

Cameron Toll
Rhyming slang for both the backside and sexual
intercourse. **Cameron Toll** = hole.
*"Any more lip from you my lad and I'll put my boot up
your Cameron Toll"* or *"Shuggie's baws were like
watermelons on account of not having had his Cameron
Toll in years."*

Caramel Log
Rhyming slang for toilet. **Caramel Log** = bog.

Chanter
A singer, normally of the pub style variety.
"Big Iain was a dooboo but he was a good chanter."
A **chanter** is also the part of a set of bagpipes that
you blow into.

Chanty

A chamberpot.
"There's a chanty under the bed that needs emptied."

Chap

To knock on something.
*"Who the hell is that **chappin** oan my door at three in the morning?"*

Chav

The Edinburgh variant of the **ned**. A **Chavette** is a female **chav**.

Chavvie

A baby.
*"Chantelle understood that another **chavvie** meant a lot of hard work and sleepless nights. On the other hand it also meant another £40 a week in benefits."*

Cheeper

A light kiss.
*"I took a right **beamer** when my Granny gave me a **cheeper** on the cheek."*

Chib

1. A knife or similar sharp instrument.
"Wee Stan was known to carry a chib on him."
2. To stab someone with a knife or similar sharp instrument.
"Please excuse Wee Stan from school as he was chibbed last night."

Ching
Cocaine.

Ching Ching
Goodbye.

Chitterin
To be shaking with the cold.

Chitterin Bite
It is a deeply held belief of all Scottish mothers that their children are extremely vulnerable to pneumonia immediately after swimming. The only known way to prevent this is to give the child a sweetie to eat upon leaving the pool. This sweetie is known as a **chitterin bite** or a **shivvery bite**.

Chokin
If you are **chokin** on something you're in a state of desperation. To be **chokin** on a can of beer means you are either very thirsty or an alcoholic.

Choob
A sycophantic person.
Also **Sook**.

Chore
To steal.
Also **Pochle**, **Knock** and **Chev**.

Chuddie

Chewing gum.
Also **Chuggie**.

Chuffed

To be happy or contented. To be pleased about something.
*"I was **chuffed** to see England get **gubbed** at the **fitba** last night."*

Chum

To accompany someone.
*"Wullie would hang around the school gates for hours in the freezing cold, in order to **chum** Sadie home."*

Chunterin

Talking.

Chuntie Heid

A stupid person.

Chute

1. The slide in a children's playground. **2.** A receptacle for the disposal of household waste in a high rise block of flats.
*"Tam arrived home a little after three o'clock in the morning to find his dinner down the **chute**."*

Clack

To chat or gossip.

Claim

To challenge someone to a fight. To make it clear to someone that you are most displeased with their actions and assure them of your intent to rectify the situation with strong words and a baseball bat. *"Haw! **Baw bag**, you're **claimed**."*

Clamp it

To shut up.

Clap

To stroke or pat something. You might **Clap** a dog.

Clart

Someone of poor personal hygiene or a dirty mind. Also **Clatty**.

Claw

To scratch at something. A **Claw Baw** is someone with their hand constantly down the front of their trousers, scratching themselves.

Click

To pull a member of the opposite sex. *"Did you get a **click** at Reflections last night?"*

Clipshear

An earwig. Also **Forky-tail**.

Clockwork Orange
Nickname given to the Glasgow underground rail network.

Close
The enclosed passage or entrance between two tenement buildings. The name comes from the close proximity of the buildings.

Clout
A hefty slap around the head.

Clype
1. To inform on or tell tales at school. **2.** A person who does this. When the **clype** leaves school they evolve into a **Grass**, which warrants hefty retribution. Also **Yop**.

Collie-Buckie
A piggy-back ride.
Also **Carry-Code** or **Cuddy-Back**.

Cooncil Gritter
Rhyming slang for the toilet. **Cooncil Gritter** = Shitter.

Cooncil Telly
The five standard terrestrial television channels are known as **cooncil telly**.
*"We'll huv tae git Sky in, there's **hee-haw** on **cooncil telly**."*

Cop Yer Whack

To die.

"It's a shame, but at least Big Jock died happy – he copped his whack at the 19th hole on the golf course."

Corbie

Old Scots dialect for a crow or raven.

Corned Beef

Rhyming slang for deaf. **Corned Beef** = deef.

Corned Beef Legs

The red mottled pattern taken on by a person's legs when they have been sitting too close to the fire.

Also known as **Fireside Tartan**.

Corned Dug

Corned beef.

Also known as **Dundee Steak**.

Corrie Fisted/Corrie Jukit

To be left-handed.

Coupon

One's face.

"I'll wipe that stupid smile right oaf his coupon."

Coupon is also a term for the football pools.

Cowp

1. To spill or throw something

"Dave managed to cowp a full glass of lager all over Rick's new jeans." Or *"After spilling a full pint of lager all over Rick's new jeans, Dave found himself being cowped over the side of the Dean Bridge."*

2. To have sexual intercourse.

"I'm taking my new burd for a curry and a couple of bellywashers then hopefully back to her bit for a cowp."

3. If a room is described as being a **cowp** it means it is in a mess.

Cow The Cuddy

To try to outdo someone or to be competitive outside a sporting event is known as **cowing the cuddy**. Similar to keeping up with the Joneses.

Crabbit

Sullen, short tempered and irritable.

Crack

Good natured and witty conversation.
"The pub's a dump but ye get good crack."

Crannie

The little finger or pinkie.

Cream Puff

Rhyming slang for a huff.

Creeshie

Creesh means fat, lard or tallow, so if something is described as being **creeshie** it means that it is covered in oil or grease.

Cry

To call.
"Whit dae ye cry that lassie thit reads the news oan telly?"

Cuddy

A horse or donkey.

Cuddy Lug

A thick ear.
"You touch they biscuits and I'll gie you a cuddy lug."

Cundie

The guttering at the side of the road.
Also **stank**.

D

Daud

A piece or lump of something.
*"Do you want a wee **daud** o' breid wi yer soup?"*

Dawner

Taken from the word 'dander' a **dawner** is a slow and meandering stroll.
*"It was a nice day so I took the **bairns** for a wee **dawner** around the shops."*

Deek

To look at something.
*"I took a wee **deek** at your motor and it looks as though the clutch is **paggered**."*
Also **Shuftie** and **Swatch**.

Deem

A woman, taken from the word Dame.

Deify

To ignore someone or pay them no heed is to sling them a **deify**.

Diddy

1. **Diddies** are ladies breasts 2. A **diddy** is a small and irritating person who thoroughly deserves a **burst mooth**.

"Get to buggery ya wee diddy."

Also **Nyaff**.

Dinger

It is unclear which part of the human anatomy contains the **dinger** but to do one's **dinger** means to lose one's temper or become temporarily insane.

Dippit

The act of doing something incredibly stupid.

"Looking for a gas leak with a match is a pretty dippit thing to do."

Dizzy

A Glasgow word meaning an instance of being stood up on a date.

"I was stood waiting outside Boots for four hours before I realised she'd given me a dizzy."

Dobber

1. A penis. 2. A slow-witted person.

Dod

A nickname given to anyone called George. Similarly anyone called Hugh is usually referred to as **Shug**, Derek is **Deek**, John becomes **Jock**, Robert is **Rab** and Alexander can be **Alec**, **Lexie** or **Sandy**.

Dog

To truant. When Glaswegian children play truant they are said to be **Dogging** school.
Also **Plunking** and **Skiving**.

Dokey

A penis.

Doll

A term of endearment or affection.
"Awright Mary Doll?"
Also **Hen**.

Dooboo

A stupid yet, at the same time, likeable person.

Dookers

Swimming trunks.

Dookin

Apple bobbing. A game played by children at hallowe'en in which they have to retrieve apples and nuts from a basin of water using only their mouths.

Dookin Fur Chips

A descriptive phrase for someone who is so grossly unattractive it looks as though they've been immersing their face in a pan of boiling hot oil.

Doolally

If someone has gone **Doolally** it means they have lost their mind.

Doonhamer

An inhabitant of Dumfries.

Doughball

A suet dumpling served in soups and stews. Also an insult directed at a person of low intelligence.

Dour

Miserable and sullen. **Dour** people not only see the glass as half empty but the remaining half has gone flat too.

Dowt

A discarded cigarette end. It is not uncommon to see **Jakeys** picking up **Dowts** from the street, removing what little tobacco is left in them and constructing a new one. These are known as **Zombie Fags**.

Dram

A shot of whisky.

Dreep

To lower oneself from a height in order to minimise the distance to the ground.
*"The **polis** agreed that the burglar had gained access from the attic and escaped by **dreeping** from the first floor window."*

Dreich
If the weather was cold, damp and miserable it might be described as **Dreich**.

Drookit
Soaked through to the skin.
*"I stood in the rain gettin **drookit** for half an hour before I saw a **Joe Baxi**."*

Drooth
A thirst. **Droothy:** Thirsty.

Dry Hump
Safe sex, in as much that both parties remain fully clothed and penetration does not take place.

Dub
A muddy puddle.

Dubbed Up
To be incarcerated in one of Her Majesty's prisons.

Duke O' Argylls
Rhyming slang for haemorrhoids. **Duke O' Argylls** = Piles.
*"Ronnie's **Duke O' Argylls** were so bad that he made history by becoming the first ever person to overdose on Preparation H."*

Dundy Money

A redundancy payment. Normally thrown on to the bar of a public house with the instructions *"Throw me out when the dundy money's finished."*

Dunt

1. To be involved in a minor collision that results in nothing more than superficial damage.
"I was just touching up my lipstick in the rear view mirror when some arsehole dunted me."
2. A small sample bag of heroin supplied free of charge.
"This dunt's on the hoose, but then it's a tenner a bag. OK?"

E

Eaksie-Peaksie

A phrase which signifies that the status quo has been maintained and everything is now equal.
*"Archie got Wullie's sister pregnant so Wullie **chibbed** Archie's wee brother. Now everything is **eaksie-peaksie**."*

Edgie

Alert for the police, security guards or potential witnesses while you carry out an illegal act.
*"Shug kept **edgie** while Boaby went in through a downstairs window."*
Edgie is a particularly Glaswegian word and the Edinburgh equivalent is **Shottie**, which comes from the Old Wild West phrase of riding shotgun, meaning to keep a look out.

Electric Soup

A playful euphemism for alcohol.
Also known as **The Singing Ginger**, **Falling Down Water**, **Vino Collapso** and **Bad Boy's Lemonade**.

Embra

Glaswegian term for Edinburgh.

F

Fanny
The female genitalia.
Also known as the **Fud**, **Flange**, **Muff** or **Growler**.

Fanny Baws
An insult.

Fash
If something is described as a **Fash** it means it is a cause of worry or concern.

Feart
Afraid. One who is afraid is known as a **feartie**.

Finicky
If someone is fussy, they are **Finicky**.

Fit
To kick something. **Fit Up The Erse:** A hefty kick up the backside.
*"If I catch you kickin that baw against my door again I'll **fit your erse**."*

Fitba
Football.

Flaky

A panic attack.
Also known as having a **Hairy Canary**.

Footer

To fiddle around with something.
Also **Ficher**.

Foosty

Old, covered in dust or mould.
*"Don't go to that cafe – their rolls are always **foosty**."*

Forfochan

A north east word for exhausted or worn out.

Full Bhoona

To do something with great vigour and
enthusiasm. To give something your full attention
and 100% effort.

Furry Boots Country

Aberdeen and surrounding areas.

Fusionless

If someone is described as **fusionless** it means
their get up and go has got up and left.

Fykie

Complicated or intricate.
Also **Scutterie**.

G

Gadgie
A typical Edinburgh term for a man of any age.

Gallus
Meaning self-confident. Also can be used to describe something stylish or impressive.
"Have you seen Boaby's new car? It's pure gallus."

Gallusses
Braces or suspenders used to hold up your trousers.

Gam
To perform fellatio. Oral sex.
Also **Gobble**.

Gammy
Something that is faulty or afflicted. A person could suffer from a **gammy** leg or a shopping trolley could have a **gammy** wheel.

Gantin
If something is **Gantin**, it means it is foul or disgusting.
"The food in here is gantin."

Geezabrek

Translated it simply means "Give me a break."

Gemme

A game.

*"Whats the gemme?", "Fancy a gemme
o' fitba.", "Fuck this fur a gemme o' soajirs."*

Gemmy

A west-coast word meaning cheeky.

Gen-Up

Taken from the word genuine, **Gen-up** is added to
the end of a statement to emphasise the fact that
you are telling the truth.

"I got five numbers in the lottery last night, gen-up."

Get It Right Up Ye

An expression of jubilation and triumph while at
the same time taking great pleasure in the defeat of
an opponent.

Gey

Very.

"It wis gey cauld last night."

Gibber

To talk incessantly and often incoherently.
Also **Haiver**, **Slaister** or **Yatter**.

Ginger

A West of Scotland term for any carbonated soft drink. Over on the East Coast you would ask for a bottle of **Juice**.

Gingy

A soft drinks bottle on which a deposit is refundable.
Also known as a **Glass Cheque**, **Jeg** or a **Rammy**.

Girn

To frown or scowl.

Gladys

Rhyming slang for shite. **Gladys Knight** = shite.

Glaikit

Stupid. **Neds** are renowned for the **Glaikit** expressions on their **Coupons**.

Glass

To assault someone with a broken glass or tumbler.

Glesca

Glasgow.

Glesca Heavy

A Glaswegian hard man.

Glesca Kiss

A head-butt. To head butt someone is to **Ram-the-Nut** or **Stoat**.

Glesca Screwdriver

A hammer.

Gob

To spit. If sufficient phlegm is expelled it is then known as a **Greener**, **Ghrocher** or **Grog**.

Goldie

Whisky.

Goonie

A dressing gown or housecoat.
*"Auld Sadie would often walk aboot the streets in nothing but her **goonie** and **baffies**."*

Gowf

The game of golf.
*"Big Jock had phoned in sick and was now off to enjoy a couple of rounds of **gowf**."*

Gowp

To throb with pain.

Granite City

Aberdeen.

Gravit

A woollen scarf.

Greet

To cry.

*"What are you **greetin** about now? I only hit you twice."*

Grippie

Tight with money.

*"There's no point asking Boab for anything – he's a **grippie** bastirt."*

Growlin At The Badger

To perform cunnilingus. Oral sex.
Also known as **Muff Diving**.

Gubbing

A humiliating defeat.

*"Scots like nothing more than seeing England get a good **gubbing** at the **fitba**."*

Guising

Similar to trick or treating. Children would traditionally go **Guising** at Hallowe'en in order to collect enough money to buy fireworks for bonfire night on November 5th.

Gutties

Cheap training shoes, often purchased from outdoor markets.

*"I wanted a pair of Nikes but my **auld dear** bought me these **gutties**."*

Also known as **Sannies**.

Gutty

A catapult.

*"Scott was such an ugly baby that his **auld dear** used to feed him with a **gutty**."*

H

Hackit
Hard faced and unattractive.

Haddie
A **haddie** is a smoked haddock but the word is more commonly used as an insult to describe someone who is useless or ineffectual.

Hairy
Derogatory name for a rough looking woman.

Hairyback
Derogatory slang for a catholic.
Also **Pape**, **Fenian** and **Left Footer**.

Hairy Twat
Playful euphemism for Edinburgh's Heriot Watt University. **Hairy Twat** = Heriot Watt.

Hameldaeme
Mythical holiday destination for skint Glaswegians. Taken literally it means home will do me.

Hank Marvin
Rhyming slang for starving.

Haud Yer Wheesht

Be quiet.

Hampden Roar

Rhyming slang for "What's the score?" or "what's up?" If someone asks "What's the **Hampden**?" they generally mean "What's going on?"

Handers

If someone asks for **Handers** it means they require assistance.

Harry Wraggs

Rhyming slang for cigarettes. **Harry Wraggs** = Fags

Hart Roastid

Fraught with worry.

Hash

To make a **Hash** of something is to make a mess of it.

Hauf 'n' a Hauf

A half pint of beer or lager and a nip of spirits. *"Ye can get a **hauf 'n' a hauf** in the Volley Arms for £2."*

Haw Haw Haw

A derisory and insincere laugh brayed by **Neds** who find endless amusement in the misfortune of others. *"Haw haw haw, ya pie"*

Haw Maws

Rhyming slang for testicles. **Haw Maws** = Baws.
"That gadgie's really starting to get on my tits. I've a damn good mind to give him a boot in the haw maws."

Healthy

Unlike the rest of the world, in Scotland this means large or prolific. For example a **Healthy** kicking is a severe assault, leaving the victim in anything but a **Healthy** state. Similarly a **Healthy** breakfast wouldn't necessarily mean grapefruit and Special K. It would more likely consist of a heart-attack-inducing plate of sausages, bacon, fried eggs, black pudding, tattie scones, fried bread and baked beans smothered in broon sauce.

Heebie-Jeebies

If you had the **Heebie-Jeebies** it would mean that you were suffering from paranoia or fear
"I don't like walking through the park at night – it gives me the heebie-jeebies."

Hee-Haw

Zero, zilch, nothing whatsoever.
"That balloon kens hee-haw aboot hee-haw."

Heels

The two slices at either end of a loaf of bread are known as the **heels**.
"Maw, can I hae a jeely piece made wi the heels?"
Also **Outsiders**.

Heid Bummer
A manager or supervisor.

Heider
To trip or throw yourself head first is known as taking a **Heider**.

Hibee
A supporter of Hibernian Football Club.

Hidin
A severe beating.
*"The auld dear found oot I was **doggin** school and she gave me a right good **hidin**."*

High Heid Yin
The owner or managing director of a company.

Hing Oot
A sexually promiscuous woman.

Hippin
A baby's nappy.

Hireys
Money.

Hirple
To limp.
*"Auld Mr Gow's **gammy** leg must be playing up again – I saw him hirpling to the shops this morning."*

Hizer
A clothes pole.
Also **Stretcher**.

Hochmagandy
Sexual intercourse between an unmarried couple.
Hochmagandy is still a stoning offence in certain
parts of Northern Scotland where this phrase is
commonly used.

Hogmanay
December 31st. From the French word *aguillaneuf,*
meaning a New Years Eve gift. This is the most
celebrated date in the Scots calendar. The stroke of
midnight on New Year's Eve is known as **The
Bells**. An old Scottish tradition is to **First-Foot**
neighbours and friends. A **First-Foot** is the first
visitor of the year and ideally should be tall, dark
and handsome in order to bring good luck to the
household.

Honest Men
An inhabitant of Ayr. Robert Burns in his poem
"Tam O' Shanter" described Ayr as being full of
honest men and bonnie lasses.

Hoochin
Although often used to imply that something is
infested with fleas or lice, the word **Hoochin**
simply means busy.

Hoor

Comes from the word whore and is used to describe a prostitute or a sexually promiscuous woman.

Hoor Maister

A sexually promiscuous man.

Howk

An ugly woman.
*"No offence, pal, but your **burd's** a **howk**."*
Also **Howler**.

Hoy

To throw something.

Huckle

To apprehend or arrest someone.
*"I was just coming out of Debenhams with a new shirt up ma **jook** when the security guards **huckled** me back into the shop."*
Also **Lift**.

Huff

A sulk.

Hughie

Vomit. So called because of the sound one makes while vomiting.

Suspected of having a chored DVD player up his jook,
Archie was huckled back into Sparky's
Electrical Superstore.

Humphie Backit

One who walks with a stoop might be described as being **Humphie Backit**.

Humpty

Bad mood or upset about something.

Hun

A supporter of Glasgow Rangers.

Hurl

A ride. If someone offers you a **hurl** up the road, it means they are offering to give you a lift home in their car.

I

Icey

Every child's delight – an ice-cream van. In some areas of Glasgow ice-cream vans sold everything from ice cream and sweets to cigarettes and heroin. The ice cream came in various forms such as a **Pokey Hat**, which was a simple ice cream cone, a **Slider** which was a scoop of ice cream between two wafers, a **Basher** which was a slider with a Tunnock's snowball thrown in for good measure and the now defunct **Black Man** which had dark chocolate covered wafers.

Ill Trickit

An Aberdonian expression meaning naughty or misbehaving.

Inversnecky

Inverness.

J

Jag

An injection.
"Ricky's dog bit me and I had to go to hospital for a jag."

Jaggy

Bad tempered and irritable.

Jakey

A down-and-out or alcoholic.
"The Grassmarket's full of jakeys trying to tap ye fur loose change."

Jambo

A supporter of Heart of Midlothian Football Club. The team are known as the Jam Tarts which is rhyming slang for Hearts.

Jammy

If someone is described as **Jammy** it means they are blessed with good luck.
"Andy's a jammy bastard. If he fell out a window, he'd go up."
Also **Spawny**.

Jannie

A school janitor.

Jeeked

Tired.

Jeely Piece

A jam sandwich.

Jellies

A street name for temazepam, an antidepressant which used to come in a gel-filled capsule. Drug users would melt the capsule and inject it into their veins. This often led to death as the gel hardened again while in the vein. For this reason doctors will now only prescribe this drug in tablet form.

Jessie

A cowardly or effeminate man.

Jobbie

Excrement.
Also **Chod**, **Keech** and **Shite**.

Joe Baxi

Rhyming slang for a taxi.
Also **Fast Black**.

Joobly

A fruit drink, frozen in a thin plastic container and then eaten like an ice lolly without the stick.

Jook

The front of your shirt, jersey or jacket.
*"After a particularly successful **chorin** spree, Dod walked out of HMV with 15 CDs up his **jook**."*

Jotters

To be given your jotters means you have been sacked from your place of employment. **Jotters** are books and it simply means to be given your books.

Judas

Rhyming slang for a carry out. **Judas** Iscariot = Carry Out
*"I'm away tae the **offie** for a **judas**."*

Jumpin Off At Haymarket

Coitus Interuptus. Contraception by means of the rhythm method.
*"I was **baw deep** then I remembered she wasn't on the pill so I had to **jump off at Haymarket**."*
Haymarket is the train station just before Edinburgh's Waverley where most trains terminate. A regional variation might be **Jumpin Off At Paisley**.

Jute City

Dundee.

K

Keks

Underpants.

"When I get hame the first thing I'm going to do is rip the wife's keks oaf. The elastic's hurtin ma legs."

Keek

To have a quick look.

Keeker

A black eye.

"Rab tried to step in and resolve a potentially volatile situation and ended up with a keeker for his troubles."

Keep The Heid

To remain calm while all around you, people are going **radge**.

Also **Retain The Loaf**.

Ken

To know, as in I **ken** that boy. = I know that boy.

Kent: Knew. I **kent** that boy = I knew that boy.

Kens: Knows. He **kens** that boy = He knows that boy.

Kettle

A wristwatch.

*According to his kettle, Archie had been waiting for
just over four hours for his burd to appear.
It would be a further two hours before he realised
she had given him a dizzy.*

Kettle Biler

Literally it means a kettle boiler. In the olden days it was cheaper to hire women than men to work in the jute mills of Dundee. The women would go out to work and upon their return, their husbands would have a cup of tea waiting for them. Unemployed men were then called **Kettle Bilers**.

Kip

1. A sleep. **2.** A bed.
"I'm away hame tae ma kip fur a kip."

Knocking Your Pan In

To be working hard.
*"I'm out at work all day **knocking my pan in** while you're lying in your kip."*

L

Labdick
A policeman who works in the drug squad.

Laddie
A boy. A girl is known as a **Lassie**.

Laldy
To do something with great energy and enthusiasm is to give it **laldy**.
"Did ye see yon drummer gein it laldy?"

Langtoun
The town of Kirkcaldy in Fife.

Lavvy
Toilet.
Also **Bog, Cludgy**.

Leather
To beat someone severely.
"The boy's getting leathered the next time I see him."
Also **Pummel, Panel**.

Lifted
To be **lifted** means to be arrested by the police.

Lillian

Rhyming slang for pish. **Lillian Gish** = Pish.

Lookin For A Brain Cell At Ibrox

A seemingly impossible task not dissimilar to searching for a needle in a haystack. Depending on your allegiance the phrase could be changed to **Lookin For A Brain Cell At Parkhead**.

Loupin

If something is described as **loupin** then it is infested with lice. A child's head, for example, or a mattress could be **Loupin**.

Lug

1. The ear. **2.** To listen to something you are not supposed to hear; to eavesdrop.

Lumber

In Glasgow getting a **Lumber** means to meet someone at a social event and hopefully shag their brains out.
"If I haven't got a lumber by 10 o'clock, I'm going home to the wife."

M

Malky

Malky Fraser was a Glaswegian debt collector who carried a cut-throat razor with which to intimidate or mutilate those who refused to pay. He now lends his name to the weapon he was famous for or the act of slashing someone's face open with a razor. If you have been **malkied** it means you have been slashed with a knife or razor.

Manky

If something is described as being **Manky** it means it is dirty. If someone is described as being **Manky** it means they are perceived as being sexually deviant

"The manky bugger wanted me to dress up as a traffic warden and chase him aroond the bedroom."

Manto

Rhyming slang for **fanny**. **Mantovani** = fanny.

Mars Bar

Rhyming slang for scar.

"Following an incident in George Square at the weekend a 22-year-old man was taken to the Royal Infirmary with a mars bar that required 35 stitches."

Mawkit

Dirty.

Melt

It is unclear whereabouts on the body a **Melt** is but if you suffered a serious assault it might be said that you had your **Melt** booted in.

Menchie

Graffiti. It's very important to a **Ned** to get a **menchie** or mention. He does this by writing or painting his name on any available surface to show his friends or enemies where he has been, thereby marking his territory.

Messages

Groceries or shopping.
"With the wife in hospital it was up to Wullie to get the messages in."

Mind

To remember.
*"**Mind** and no forget."*

Minger

A sexually repellent individual. Yet another Scottish word that has now been adopted by the rest of the UK.

Mingin

Smelly or untidy.
*"Auld Archie's hoose was **mingin**."*

Mink

Someone who is dirty or has a dirty mind.
Also **Clart**, **Manky**.

Moothie

A mouth organ or harmonica.

Morn

Tomorrow.
*"I'll see you the **morn**."*
The **Morn's mornin** would be tomorrow morning.

Muckle

Large.
*"PC Murdoch was famous for his **muckle** feet."*

*"Here you, ya manky bugger. This isnae
a cludgy ye ken."*

N

Napper
The head.

Nash
To hurry or run away quickly.
"Nash! Here come the polis."

Nat King Cole
Rhyming slang for sex. **Nat King Cole** = Hole.
"Jimmy had been winchin Gayle for yonks but still hadn't had his Nat King Cole."

Neb
The **Neb** is the nose. If someone is **Nebby** it means they are nosey.

Necky
To be cheeky or take liberties.

Ned
Neds are to be found all over Scotland but it is in Glasgow that the best examples are to be found. Some people think that **Ned** is an acronym of **N**on-**E**ducated **D**elinquent but it is more likely taken from the word Ne'er-do-well. They are extremely anti-social young men who enjoy nothing more than getting drunk or taking drugs

Unlike other primates, the Burberry Ape has little in common with human beings.

and intimidating members of the general public. They are easily recognisable by their **sovs**, brightly coloured tracksuits tucked into their socks, training shoes and baseball caps which they like to wear at funny angles. They also have a love of designer labels, in particular Burberry. Those who favour this label are punningly called Burberry Apes. Female **Neds** are known as **Sengas** and are virtually indistinguishable from the males although they do speak in a lower tone of voice.

Neebs
A Fife expression meaning neighbour or friend.

Neep
A turnip. Commonly found as part of the traditional Scottish dish, Haggis, **Neeps** and **Tatties**.
Also **Tumshie**.

Nip
A shot of whisky, vodka, rum, brandy, gin etc. Any alcoholic spirit.
*"Dave would've been fine if he stuck to pints but once he hit the **nips** he went **radge**."*

Nookie Badge
A love bite; a hickey.

O

Offie

An off-licence.

Offski

Leaving quickly.
"I've time for a quick pint then I'm offski."

Oxter

An armpit.

P

Paddy's Market

An untidy or disorganised place would be likened to **Paddy's Market**.
*"Away and tidy yer room – it's like **Paddy's Market** in there."*

Pagger

A fight.
Also **Swedge**.

Pan Breid

Rhyming slang for dead. **Pan Breid** = Deid.

Paps

Breasts.

Partan

A **partan** is a crab. If someone has a **partan** face it means they are scowling or sneering.

Peely-Wally

Pale or sickly.
*"Aye he looked a bit **peely-wally** when I saw him last."*

Peenge

To moan or complain.

Peenie

An apron.

Pee The Bed

A dandelion. The name comes from an urban myth held true by children that touching the flowering weed would make you wet the bed.

Peever

A children's game similar to hopscotch.

Persian Rugs

Rhyming slang for drugs.
Also **Sniffer Dugs**.

Petted Lip

If someone is described as having a petted lip it means they are in a **huff** or sulking.

Piece

A sandwich.
Also **Sanger** or **Swedger**.
A snack or sweetie given to schoolchildren to eat during their morning break is known as a **play piece**.

Plampher

A **plampher** is a sexual deviant who steals ladies underwear from washing lines or laundry baskets.
Also known as a **Snowdropper**.

Plank

To set something down.

*"Just **plank** yersel in that chair and take it easy."*

Playgie

A playground.

Plook

A spot or zit. Someone suffering from bad acne might be called **Plooky**.

Pochle

To steal something.

*"Did you **pochle** that car stereo?"*

Podger

To have sexual intercourse.

Poke

A sheet of paper fashioned into a cone to carry chips or sweeties in.

Polis

The police.

*"**Shottie**, here come the **polis**."*

Also **Boaby**.

Poor Oot

It is traditional at a Scottish wedding for the bridegroom or best man to throw coins from the window of the car as they leave the church for the reception. Waiting children then rush forward to collect the coins.
Also known as a **Scramble**.

Potted

Rhyming slang for dead. **Potted Seed** = Deid.

Pram Posse

A gathering of two or more single mothers. Usually found in shopping precincts or queuing outside the post office on a Monday morning.

Puddock

A frog.

Puff

By oneself. To be alone.
"Friday night and here I am on my puff."
Can also mean life, as in:
"He was sent to Bar-L for the remainder of his puff."

Puggled

To be exhausted.

Puggy

Fruit machine or one-armed bandit.
"I just won ten bar oan the puggy."

Pump

To have sexual intercourse.

Punt-up

To assist someone in scaling a wall by cupping your hands together as a foothold.
Also known as a **Hoisty** or a **Leggie**.

Pure Quality

A phrase which indicates something is of the highest standard.
*"This gear's **pure quality** by the way."*

Pus

The mouth.
*"Shut yer **pus**!"*
Also **Geggie** or **Gub**.

R

Rab Ha
1. The legendary Glasgow greedy-guts. 2. To be likened to **Rab Ha** means you have a large appetite.

Radge
An east coast expression meaning mad or crazy.

Rake
An unspecified yet large number or amount.
*"We are expecting a **rake** of complaints about this book."*

Randan
If you were going out on the **Randan** you would be going out to paint the town red.
*"Lock up your daughters, the boys are on the **randan**."*

Red Biddy
A popular beverage among the **Jakey** community, its ingredients consist of cheap red wine and methylated spirits.

Rift
To burp or belch.

Right Off The Reel
Straight away. If, for example, you were waiting to see the doctor and you were seen quickly, you might say you were taken **right off the reel**.

Rub Shop
A brothel masquerading as a massage parlour.
*"The **polis** raided Auld Dora's **rub shop** and **lifted** three priests and a high court Judge."*

Rubber Ear
To ignore someone.
Also **Dinghy**.

S

Sap

Someone with little or no physical strength; a
coward.
*"Away ye go ya big Jessie! Dinnae be feart of him –
he's a sap."*

Scabby Wean's Heid

A hypothetical meal consisting of the head of a
child with a skin disorder. This unappetising dish
is used to emphasise how hungry you are.
"Ah'm that hungry I could eat a scabby wean's heid."
A variation could be a **scabby hoarse between two
pishy matresses**.

Scaffy

A road sweeper. The name comes from the word
scavenger.

Schemie

Derogatory name for an inhabitant of an inner city
housing scheme. Stereotypical **schemies** will wear
shell suits, have children with behavioural
problems and more often than not own a bull
terrier.

Young Charlie took a beamer when his Auld Dear found
a rake of scuddy books under his scratcher.

Scooby

Rhyming slang for clue. **Scooby Doo** = Clue.
*"I'm sorry but I haven't got a **scooby** as to what you're haivering about."*

Scoosh

Soft drinks.

Scran

Can mean both food or the act of eating food.
*"Any **scran** in the hoose? I'm pure **Hank Marvin**."*

Scratcher

A bed.

Scud

A hefty slap.

Scuddy

Naked. Pornographic magazines are known as **Scuddy Books**.

Scunner

To sicken yourself or others.

See You Jimmy

A catch phrase made famous by English comedians attempting a Scottish accent. A **See You Jimmy** hat is a tartan tammy with a ginger wig sewn into the back. Other nonsensical phrases include **Och Aye The Noo** and **Jings, Crivvens, Help Ma Boab**.

Semmit
A vest.

Sesh
A prolonged period of heavy drinking.
"Don't wait up for me sweetheart. I'm going on a sesh."

Shan
Cruel or unfair.

Shareen
Rhyming slang for fanny. **Shareen Nanjani** = Fanny.

Shelter Belter
An increasingly common sight in city centres on Friday and Saturday nights. A **Shelter Belter** is a young lady in a state of intoxication having sex in a bus shelter.

Sherakin
If your boss gave you a **sherakin** he would have bawled you out.
"I got a right sherakin for putting the wrong date on those invoices."

Sheriff's Badge
Rhyming slang for **Radge**.

Shillpit

Skinny or malnourished.

Shining Bright

Rhyming slang for **That Will Be Right**. A sarcastic response to an unbelievable statement.

Shite It

To be afraid; to lose your bottle.

Shoogle

To shake or wobble.
*"**Shoogle** that pram a wee bit to stop the **bairn** frae greetin."*
In Glasgow the old trams were known as **Shooglies**.

Shoot The Craw

To leave, depart.

Shop Front

Rhyming slang for **Cunt**.

Single Fish

Rhyming slang for **Pish**.

Single/Supper

When ordering in a Scottish chip shop, anything with chips is known as a **Supper**, while an item without chips is a **Single**.

Skag
Heroin.

Skelly Eyed
Description of someone who has a squint or lazy eye.

Skelp
A slap with an open hand.

Skite
To slip or slide on an oily, icy or wet surface.
*"It's gey icy oot there. I just went **skiting** doon the path on my arse."*
Skite can also mean to hit someone.

Skitters
Diahorrea.

Slaister
A messy eater; one who dribbles.
*"Look at ye, ye've soup a' doon yir shirt, ya **slaister**."*
A **slaister** can also be someone who talks a lot of nonsense.

Slater
A wood louse.

Slug
If you were asking someone for a drink from their bottle you might ask for a **slug** or a **chug**.

Smack Heid
A heroin addict.

Sneck
A door snib.
*"**Mind** an put the **snib** on before ye go to bed."*

Snell
Snow.
Also **Snedge**.

Snotter
Nasal mucus. A runny nose is a **Snottery Beak**.

Soap Dodger
Derogatory term for a Glaswegian. It is a slur on their supposedly poor personal hygiene.

Soapy Bubble
Rhyming slang for **Trouble**.

Sov
A gold sovereign ring. This ungainly item of jewellery is favoured by **Neds**.
Also known as **Highland Bling**.

Spam Valley
A middle class area.

Spaver
A small fragment of wood, glass or metal stuck in one's finger.
Also **spale** or **skelf**.

Spawny
Lucky.

Spew
To spew is to vomit. It can also mean to curse one's own bad luck.
"I won £50 on the horses then got a phone bill for £60. I was spewing."

Spraff
To talk.

Square Go
A fair fight between two people involving no weapons.

Stair
The common stairwell and landings of a tenement building.
"We've got too many moaning auld folk in oor stair."

Stakey
A **chib** with a long blade.

Stappit
To be full to bursting.
"I couldn't eat another bite. I'm absolutely stappit."

Stauner

An erection.
Also **Steamer**.

Steamie

A launderette. The talk of the **Steamie** is an expression meaning the subject of gossip.

Stoat The Baw

A phrase used to describe a man who is in a relationship with a girl dangerously younger than himself.

Stoat

1. To hit something with your head. **2.** To walk.
"Whae wis that lassie I saw ye stoatin' aboot wi last night?"

Stoater

Anything impressive or worthy of praise is described as a **Stoater**.
"Did ye see Tam's new burd? She's a real stoater."

Stookie

A plaster cast. To **stookie** someone is to break their arm or leg.

Stoor

Dust or fluff.
Also known as **Ooze** or **Caddis**.

Stoorie
To hurry; to run at great speed.

Stooshie
Protest or uproar.
"There was a big stooshie when the high heid yin telt us we wurnae getting a pay rise."

Stowed Oot
If a place is described as **Stowed Oot** it is extremely busy.

Swack
An Aberdonian phrase meaning fit or supple.

Sweetie Wifie
A **Sweetie Wifie** is a man who has all the characteristics of an old woman. **Sweetie Wifies** enjoy partaking in idle gossip, watching soap operas or, in the most extreme circumstances, playing bingo.

Swick
To cheat, con or swindle.

Switherin
Unsure or undecided.
"I'm switherin as to whether I should go to Ibiza or Benidorm this year."

Sybie
A spring onion.

T

Tadger

A small penis. A large penis might be called a
Walloper.

Tan

1. If you were to **tan** a window you would be
smashing it. **2.** If you were to **tan** a dozen cans you
would have drunk all twelve of them. **3.** If you
were to **tan** someone's jaw, you would have hit it
hard enough to leave them with a mark resembling
sunburn.

Tap

To borrow something.
*"Can I **tap** ten **bar** until pay-day?"*

Tarry

Rhyming slang for cannabis. **Tarry Rope** = Dope.

Tartan Army

The name given to the die-hard followers of the Scottish national football team. The **Tartan Army** can be easily identified by their kilts, Scotland tops and **See You Jimmy** hats. You would be hard pushed to identify a sober member of the **Tartan Army** though, unlike English fans, these ambassadors of Scotland are famous for their good behaviour and, as such, are welcomed all over the world.

Tattie

A potato.

Tattie-Bogle

A scarecrow.

Tattie Water

Semen.

Tea Jenny

Someone who drinks a lot of tea.

Tex Ritter

Rhyming slang for diahorrea. **Tex Ritter** = Skitter.

The Man

A figure of authority. A misbehaving child might hear the dreaded cry from their **Auld Dear**:
*"Stop that! Here's **the man** coming."*

In 1990, the Tartan Army were sent to Iraq.
They found no sign of chemical weapons or Saddam
Hussein but they did bump into Freddie Mercury and a
healthy amount of electric soup.

Thrapple
The throat or windpipe

Tim
A Roman Catholic; a Celtic supporter.

Tin Pail
Rhyming slang for **jail**.

Toley
A small **jobbie**.

Torn Faced
Miserable or in a bad mood.

Tottie
Very small.

Trackies
A tracksuit, the uniform of the **ned**.

Tro
An extremely abbreviated form of cheerio.

Troops
Fellow **Neds**.
"Awright troops?"

Turkish Delight
Rhyming slang for **shite**.

V

Varicose Veins
Rhyming slang for **weans**.

W

Wabbit
Feeling slightly off colour.

Walk In The Lobby
Rhyming slang for **jobbie**.

Wallies
False teeth.

Wally Dugs
Originally **Wally Dugs** were small ornamental statues of dogs, but the phrase has been broadened to incorporate any ornament or knick-knack one might keep on a mantelpiece.

Wean
A child, literally meaning 'wee one'.

Wee Man
A child or anyone under five feet in height.

Weegie
A native of Glasgow.

Well-Skelped Erse

If someone is described as having a face like a
well-skelped erse they have a ruddy complexion,
normally associated with the over-consumption of
alcohol.

Wet Penny

The small dark circular stain found on the crotch
of men's light coloured trousers caused by
insufficient shaking following a visit to the toilet.
*"Is that a **wet penny** in your poacket or did ye just
pish yer keks?"*

Wide

To be streetwise or savvy

Wide-O

Someone who believes themselves to be streetwise
or savvy. This, of course, is rarely the case and a
Burst Mooth is often needed to convince them
otherwise.

Wifie

A middle aged woman.

Winchin

To be going steady with someone of the opposite
sex.

Shuggie McDuff got his jotters fae work.
Isa MacDougal's eldest laddie chibbed a boaby and got
8 years in the big hoose wi the wee windaes. Senga
Mcleod's workin in a rub shoap and fur the fourth night in
a row some clatty plampher's chored my keks oaf the rope
in the back green. This is Doreen Gow, nebby windae-
hinger fur News at 10.

Windae Hingin

To lean out of ones window and gossip with a neighbour is known as **Windae Hingin**. These are normally old women who spend a great deal of time with their noses in others people's business

Windae Licker

Someone who is feeble minded or mentally deficient.

Wired In

If someone told you to get **wired in** you would be expected to help yourself to as much as you would like.

"There's plenty sandwiches, sausage rolls, cakes and biscuits, so get wired in."

Workin Yer Ticket

Pushing your luck or being involved in a scam.

Y

Ya Bass

Often seen scrawled across walls beneath a street gang's name, for example 'TONGS YA BASS'. Despite popular belief, this does not simply mean 'you bastard' but is in fact an old Gaelic war cry.

Ya Dancer

An exclamation of triumph and joy, often heard in bookies.

Yak

The eye.
"Watch whit yer daein wi that stick. Ye nearly had ma yak oot."

Yer Maw

A good way to start a fight is to make a disparaging comment about someone's mother. If you cannot think of anything particularly scathing or offensive it is perfectly acceptable to simply say **"Yer Maw"** and the insultee will understand and most probably engage you in physical combat anyway.

Yer Tea's Oot

If someone tells you, '**Yer Tea's Oot**' it means they are challenging you to fight.

Yokin Time

The hour at which you start work. **Lousin Time** is the hour at which you go home.

Yon Time

An unspecified yet late hour of the day.
*"I'll no be hame till **yon time**."*

Yonks

An unspecified yet lengthy period of time.